The
GoodBooze

RECIPE ·and·
COOKBOOK

The GoodBooze

RECIPE ·and· COOKBOOK

PALADIN PRESS
BOULDER, COLORADO

James C. Krohn

The Good Booze Recipe and Cookbook
by James C. Krohn

Copyright © 1988 by James C. Krohn

ISBN 13: 978-0-87364-450-1
Printed in the United States of America

Published by Paladin Press, a division of
Paladin Enterprises, Inc.
Gunbarrel Tech Center, 7077 Winchester Circle
Boulder, Colorado 80301 USA, +1.303.443.7250

Direct inquiries and/or orders to the above address.

Visit our website at www.paladin-press.com

Warning

While the methods and materials described in this publication have been proven to produce good, safe alcohol for consumption, neither Paladin Press nor the author assumes any responsibility for the use or misuse of this information. Neither Paladin Press nor the author assume liability for the products of any distillery so constructed or operated. Be advised that the reader is responsible for adherence to local, state, or federal laws governing the private production, distribution, or sale of alcohol.

Contents

Introduction 1

Chapter 1 Getting Started 3

Chapter 2 Building the Still 11

Chapter 3 Making the Booze 17

Chapter 4 Bourbon, Gin, and Other
Flavored Liquors 27

Chapter 5 Safeguards 31

Appendix Equipment and Supplies. 35

Introduction

I like the memory of those days when I would come home from work, tired, hot, and thirsty. I'd set the "brain bag" down, throw down my hat, and look for a cool drink. As I would take a glass and drop in some ice cubes, I would imagine those of all the many generations before me who had done the same thing. Maybe some poured their wine from an old cask; others, more lucky than me, could merely clap their hands and a servant would appear.

Up until 1967, I was content with the alcohol that was commonly for sale on the market. Then, I came to a turning point in my life: I tasted *good* booze for the first time! It was smooth, pleasant, and—holy cow!—I didn't get a hangover from it!

Like others, I assumed liquor distilling was a complex, involved operation understood by only master chemists and professional distillers. I found out that wasn't so as I began asking around.

More correctly, the process involves only a few basic principles. The process is nearly the same for making beer, wine, and hard liquor. The mash is "set," and then the yeast goes to work, converting sugars and starches into alcohol. Thereafter, the distillation is merely a thermal action whereby the alcohol is boiled off, leaving the water and residues behind.

In this brief book, we're going to walk you through the steps involved in setting up a still and running off a batch of clear alcohol (sugar alky). By the time you have read through this short discussion, you will have discovered the secrets of making *good* booze.

1.

Getting Started

The alcohol you and I drink, be it from the can, bottle, or cask, has ethyl alcohol in it. This is also known as grain alcohol, or C_2H_5OH. I have found that a combination of *pure* ethyl alcohol and clean water makes a very pleasant drink. The liver goes to work on the alcohol and breaks it down into blood sugars. The rest of the circulating alcohol serves to impair blood circulation to the brain by impeding the oxygen flow, giving that pleasant, relaxing feeling.

Clean alcohol is what spoiled me, for I learned to like it and appreciate it. Stateside alcohol (alcohol that has been produced by commercial alcohol manufacturers in the United States), on the other hand, will give a person a headache and hangover that is painful. Alcoholic beverages, for example, were sent to servicemen in Vietnam "preserved" with so much formaldehyde in them—listed on the can—that men would have diarrhea after drinking two cans of the stuff! In this book, we're going to cover the technique of making *clean* alcohol.

There are other kinds of alcohol about, and we will avoid them. There's methyl alcohol (methanol), which is fit for industrial use only. If consumed, it will make the drinker sick, blind, crazy, and, finally, dead! Propyl alcohol (propanol) is commonly available in a permanently undrinkable form, isopropyl alcohol. There are many other types of alcohols, but we're interested only in ethyl alcohol here.

Using yeast is the quickest and most efficient way of making our alcohol. There are other laboratory and plant methods that can be used, but they are more costly and involved. The yeast is added to water and some form of sugar. In days gone by, people used grapes. Later, others tried anything that had starch in it, such as potatoes and grain.

The yeast, provided the conditions are right, will attack the sugar or starch product. As the yeast grows, it converts the sugars into alcohol. An important by-product of this reaction is carbon dioxide. Remember this and keep the mash lids tightly closed.

There are two kinds of conditions under which various microbes like to operate. One is *aerobic*, where the "little bugs" like the air and the oxygen (O_2) it contains. Yeast doesn't like air, working only in an *anaerobic* (airless) environment while it converts the materials to alcohol. Earlier, carbon dioxide (CO_2) was mentioned as a by-product; the yeast will use this as a buffer to the outside air. If air gets into the working mash, it will kill the yeast and stop the operation. That's why it is so important to keep the mash lids tightly closed.

The yeast, working in the dark, warm, moist mash, will continue working until one of its resources—either sugar, CO_2, nutrients, or temperature—gives out. The unused sugar and spent yeast will then settle to the bottom of the mixture as dregs.

Let's walk through the steps of setting up a modest booze operation. For the sake of simplicity, I'm going to describe the setup I had and give you some facts and statistics to consider.

THE WORKROOM

The first thing you need is a room where you can set up the operation. If you're going to make small amounts, perhaps you can do it right in your kitchen. Otherwise, you need to set aside a dedicated area for the batch.

In terms of running off a batch, you will need the room for three to four weeks. Once you have the area located, four things are needed to do this job quickly.

1. Electricity (preferably 220V to drive the heaters or hot plates)
2. Water (which can be run in by a garden hose)
3. Controlled room heat (to keep the working yeast comfortably warm)
4. Ventilation (to avoid build-up of an explosive/ flammable atmosphere)

I set aside a room large enough for ten 26-gallon plastic garbage cans. Mash would be set in these containers and then covered. Each can was well rinsed and then filled with just ten inches of water.

WATER

If you are truly bent on making excellent booze, I strongly recommend you use "raw" water, that is to say, water from a well, spring, clean creek, or snowmelt. Many chemicals harmful to yeast growth have been added to "treated, purified" water (such as chlorine, alum, acids, and who knows what else). Should you have well water in your house, fine. Just be sure you are not taking water from a water softener should one be installed.

WATER TEMPERATURE AND YEAST

The plastic cans are now each holding ten inches of water. Oftentimes the water is cool, possibly chilly. At that temperature, it's far too cold for the yeast, and you need to let the water come up to room temperature. For setting mash, the water should be above 70°F and not warmer than 88°F. (Disregard what it says on the yeast container. We're not making bread dough— we want two weeks' work from the yeast.)

We've got our materials gathered and we're ready for the next step.

SETTING THE MASH

First, a common pail is needed to measure out the sugar; a three-gallon bucket will do. Heap the pail with sugar and pour it into the mash barrel. Stir the sugar so it doesn't cake and settle on the bottom. Yeast cannot get down into packed or settled sugar. Some people try to avoid having to clean the mash barrels by lining them with plastic bags. Often, there is too much force or improper seating, causing the bags to tear and make an even greater mess. I avoid using the plastic bags and suggest you do the same.

The water and sugar mixture is now close to room temperature. The sugar can be stirred or moved around with a stick or canoe paddle. Once the chill is out of the water, the yeast can be added.

I buy regular Fleischmann's dry yeast in pint cans. Any *cooking* yeast will do. The exact amount of yeast needed depends on the age of the yeast (the date on the yeast package will indicate this). If the yeast is fairly fresh, you can use about a cupful per 26 gallons of mash. Older yeast may be added by the *heaping* cupful. Continue measuring out a ration of yeast for each barrel of mash you are setting.

Now look back at the first cans of mash. You will see that they are brimming with foam! That foaming action is the reason you start with only ten inches of water.

Finish distributing the yeast, and get ready for the next step.

We have one more ingredient to add before we are done setting the mash: water softener, which has materials in it that the yeast greatly favors and that will ultimately improve the sugar conversion to alcohol. Add about three-quarters of a cup of water softener to each mash container. The water softener does not affect the taste of your final product. Set the lids on all the mash barrels and wait for the foaming to settle down.

The last part of setting mash is to add water. As the foaming has died down, water can be added to bring each mash container to the full mark.

This part gets tricky. If you suddenly add more cold water to the working yeast, the yeast may be shocked and killed. On the other hand, if you don't add the rest of the water soon enough, the yeast may suffocate and die. Often, I keep water on the stove and pour it into my roof cistern to take the chill out of the water. You might want to add boiling water to the fresh water before adding it to the mash.

To summarize: set the mash by combining water, sugar, yeast, water softener, and then more water. Once the barrels are full, cap the lids *tightly! We leave them alone for ten days.*

As the yeast works in the mash, it has a narrow temperature tolerance, working best at temperatures of 84°–88°F. Should the temperature fall below 70°F the yeast will be stopped and later killed. If the mash temperature rises above 88°F you've exceeded the upper temperature range for the yeast. Remember, you want to coax two weeks' worth out of the yeast.

You might wonder how you'll know when the mash is done, when it stops working, and whether you can take a look. (Remember the CO_2?)

Be sure to wait ten days before you take a peek. When the yeast has stopped working (bubbling) and the mash is starting to clear, you'll know the mash is ready to cook. The next job is to build the still.

2.

Building the Still

I bought four five-gallon pressure cookers and had the top lips cut off two of them and the bottoms cut out of the other pair. The large pieces were heli-arced (welded) together to give me two complete ten-gallon cookers. Though buying four pressure cookers may seem like you're spending a lot of money, consider that it will speed up the process. After all, you don't want to be cooking booze for a whole month. Rather, you wanted to have the cooking out of the way within a week. At the time that I bought mine, a still would pay for itself after the first batch was cooked up. You, however, can select the size and number of cookers *you* will be comfortable with. If you choose one pressure cooker to sit on the kitchen stove, fine!

The two cookers I made were modified even further: I removed the safety valves and pressure gauges. The center hole held a rubber O-ring and my thermometer.

The side hole would accept a union for the future cooling coil.

I bored a hole at the bottom of each cooker and tapped it to accept a gate-type drain valve. It would hold the pressure and still allow me to quickly drain the pot.

What kind of thermometer, you ask? I like the lab-type alcohol—not mercury—thermometer that's marked in degrees centigrade. These are available at scientific and lab supply houses. (Also, some college chemistry departments have "country stores" where these may be purchased.) You will need one for each cooker, and a spare (for the one you're going to break— it always happens!).

Take the new thermometer out of its holder and take a minute to learn how to read it. Study it closely so that you know what temperature each mark represents.

Lubricate the rubber O-ring with medicinal oil and seat it in the cooker cover. (Medicinal oil is a flavorless oil that adds no foreign taste to your finished product— you can find this at any pharmacy.) Then lubricate the bottom of the thermometer and ease it into the O-ring. Seat it only far enough so that when you set the cover down, the thermometer won't touch anything and break. Now, take the cardboard tube that the thermometer came in, and trim it so it sits around the thermometer and shows 80° and up. This will allow you to read the mash temperature accurately.

The next job is to make the copper cooling coils. The fitting (to be found in the cooker cover), the nut, and the tubing have to be the same corresponding size. I prefer three-eighths-inch to seven-sixteenths-inch I.D. (inside diameter) soft-drawn copper tubing. Soft-drawn tubing is more forgiving when you expand it and hang it up. The I.D. is dependent on the heat output of your electric heaters.

I had four 5,000-watt hot plates under my two ten-gallon cookers. The copper lines could handle the resulting flows. It's best to start out with *high heat* and then cut back the heat as the pot's temperature climbs. Watch the flow out of the copper line and make sure it's clean and not sputtering. The rule is to avoid excessive pressure (and a rise in temperature) as the booze is being cooked off.

The length of copper tubing used for each cooker can be about eight feet long. The diameter of the coils is not important; what matters is that all parts of the coil slope downward.

Once you have loaded a cooker and turned on the heat, the mash begins to cook (boil) in the cooker. Alcohol has a lower boiling temperature than water and is the first element to boil off as vapor. This vapor then travels through the copper cooling coil and returns as a liquid. You have a choice of cooling the coil(s) by air or by water (the preferred method). The alcohol can be collected at the end of the coil(s).

At this point, you've got the heaters in place and the open cooker sitting on the heaters. The cover sits ready with its thermometer and coil fitting installed. Finally, the copper coil sits ready to be attached to the cooker cover. Are you ready?

No, not quite. You have to clean the entire apparatus

before you start cooking. If you don't clean all this new equipment, the drinkers will later come down with the darnedest case of diarrhea you've ever seen!

Take the pail and measure out a few tablespoons of vinegar and a teaspoon of salt. Fill the pail with water and dissolve everything. Now, preferably with aluminum wool, scrub out the cooker. With a funnel and more cleaning solution, the cooling coil is also rinsed out. You're now learning the "first secret" of making good booze: *keeping the equipment clean!*

The pot and coil are then rinsed three times and taste tested for cleanliness. It's usually quite clean after the third freshwater rinse.

One very important note: *never use soap to clean your still!* Using soap to clean your still is another good way to ruin your booze and your still. (You may as well throw the still out once soap touches it. Most soaps are alkaline in nature and are darn near impossible to neutralize after they have seeped into the aluminum.) The clean pots are now placed on the heaters.

You've got one more job to do before loading the pots. On the lip of the pot or hidden on the cover is a long, thin O-ring. Remove this O-ring and lubricate it with some medicinal oil. This lubrication will help the O-ring to seal the cooker and keep the alcohol vapors inside.

Our ten days of waiting aren't up yet, so let's consider the following question and answer exchange:

Q. "What's the capacity of all these cans here?"
A. "Two hundred seventy-six gallons."

Q. "How much sugar do you buy?"

A. "I've been buying 240 pounds each time."

Q. "What kind of yield do you get?"

A. "About 9 to 9 1/2 percent."

Q. "Is that good or bad?"

A. "It doesn't sound impressive, since the other guys claim they get 10, 11, and 12 percent. That doesn't discount bragging or 'pushing the thermometers' a little hard."

Q. "What is the hardest part in cooking booze?"

A. "Getting set up is the hardest. After that, everything is very easy, except for cleaning the bottles. That to me is always a pain."

Q. "So, from your 276 gallons, how much would you bottle?"

A. "It averages out at 22 gallons."

Q. "Is that uncut, or cut with water?"

A. "Uncut."

Q. "That would come to how many fifths?"

A. "About 110 fifths."

Q. "From start to finish, how long does it take for one batch to be run off?"

A. "Everything? Figure about three weeks without interfering with your job."

Q. "Explain."

A. "Well, first you set the mash. That's ten days to two weeks. The 20-gallon capacity of the still can cook off all the mash in four runs within a week. I set the pots up so my wife can turn the heat on later in the morning. By the time I get home from work, the first is beginning to run off. There's still time for a second twenty gallons of mash to cook down before bedtime."

Q. "Could you cook more booze with the equipment you have?"

A. "Oh, certainly! I could set more mash as soon as the barrels are emptied, but I don't."

Q. "Why?"

A. "There's no point in making the bootlegger's fatal mistake: getting greedy!"

3.

Making the Booze

In the distilling process, you are merely using heat to thermally extract the alcohol from the solution—there is *no* chemical reaction. The clean pots are set up, the heaters are ready to go, and the coils sit ready in the large tank.

THE FIRST RUN

Ten days have passed now, and you're ready to look at the mash to see if it's ready. If you peek in all the mash containers and see that three have finished working and are starting to clear, that's good! That means we're ready to start the first run.

The entire quantity of *clear* mash will be cooked down. With each potful (after reaching the prescribed temperature), collect the distilled fluid into a clean barrel. When the first run temperature is reached, turn

17

off the heat, dump out the pots, and refill them. Once again, the heat is turned on.

Keep this up until all the good mash has been cooked. Each time the fluid is collected, the process is called a "run." Your main limitation (and concern from now on) will be the temperature. The maximum cooking temperature allowed during the first run is 96°C.

This is the second secret to making good booze: *never exceed your temperatures!*

If by chance you should ever exceed your temperature for that run, shut off the power, de-pressurize, dump out the cooker, and clean it out. The jug of burned booze can be thrown out (don't throw out the whole run!). There is no saving or re-cooking "burned" booze; once a jug is ruined, it's ruined.

Rather than making a mess by bailing mash in a pail and then pouring it into the cooker, I use a small electric driven pump. Two lengths of garden hose allow me to pump the clearing mash from the barrels cleanly into the cookers. (Spilled mash is very messy and sticky, and it stinks!) Check the drain valves to make sure they're closed. Insert the suction hose into the clearing mash only a few inches. Avoid sucking up any of the dregs, as doing so causes excessive (uncontrollable) foaming in the cookers.

Fill the cooker no higher than eight inches from the top. The clear mash tends to froth as it is, and any higher levels will send mash through your condensing coils. That becomes a difficult mess to clean out!

The pot is now filled with mash to eight inches from the top. Check the thermometer; the bulb is to be at the same height as the vapor port. Install the cover on the cooker securely. Hook up the copper coil line. Now, turn the power on high.

Here is a rule to learn and observe: From this point on, *there can be no smoking or drinking!* The potential for accidents is too great.

During the first run, six to seven hours may pass before a pot is done. All you have to do is watch the temperature (below 96°C) and verify that the fluid keeps flowing out the coil's port.

If the fluid stops flowing, the cooling coil may have become plugged. Shut off the power immediately and clear the obstruction.

Safety in Opening the Still

As that pot bubbles merrily away, it is something you must respect. There's a lot of energy held underneath that cover.

As your temperature comes up to the limit (96°C for the first run), or when you have to stop the still and open it, you must be very careful! Once the power is off, you can disconnect the cooling coil safely and, if necessary, open the drain valve safely. It's the cover you have to watch out for!

When there is no longer any gas discharge from the cover's fitting, you can be reasonably assured you have *disarmed* the cooker. That's when you can take off the cover to see what's left.

On the other hand, if a person is impatient and unlocks that cover too soon, he/she will get a bath of scalding mash! Additionally, the cover will take off and bounce off the ceiling! (I was in a hurry one day, and found this out!)

Need I say more?

Most of the time, after you've become accustomed to your still, you'll normally cut the heater power and merely flip the drain valve(s) open. Doing so takes care of dangerous pressures.

THE SECOND RUN

The first run usually takes the longest time, with the second, third, and fourth each taking far less time.

After the first run (and each run thereafter) is completed, the still has to be cleaned. (You do *not* have to clean after every potful.) The collected first run is now poured into the clean cookers. At this stage, the fluid is extremely clear and there isn't quite so much of it.

If you are concerned with efficiency and getting as much alcohol as possible from the process, you should then take care to watch the amounts of sugar and yeast, as well as water temperature, for this mash. Later, when cooking the runs, you may prefer to watch as the temperature limit for that run is approached. For the second run, for example, the temperature limit is 94°C. You may decide to cut back on the power (heat) and let the temperature slowly approach the limit. Now, you *must* watch the thermometer and the discharge spout; when the alcohol stops coming, it's done! On the other hand, if the power remains on high (as it does when I cook it), the temperature is going to soar when that potful is done. You have to remain alert! As the batch proceeds through the runs, the time lag shortens as the alcohol pours out faster.

What's a good way to collect the alcohol? I usually have a plastic funnel with a large wad of clean cotton to filter and guide the liquid into a jug.

The jugs are usually "scrounged" from the local soft drink bottler; these are the castoff syrup jugs. Clean them with the same vinegar/salt/water solution and give them three good rinses and the ever-reliable taste test.

Once again, during the second run, you have the same things to watch for: constant fluid flow and the temperature. During the second run, your maximum temperature is 94°C. That's two degrees less than the first run.

The first run is now bailed into the cookers. The reason for this is that the pump and hoses used for the mash are dirty and will contaminate this fluid.

The second run is completed, as now we prepare for the third run.

THE THIRD RUN

Each run is a gradual purification of the alcohol. We are removing more and more of the water and contaminants with each step.

Once again, the pots and coils are cleaned in preparation for refilling. The second run fluid is poured into the pots, the covers are installed, the lines are hooked up, and the power is turned on. Gallon jugs with funnels and cotton await the distillate.

You may have some questions:

Q. "Why four runs?"

A. "That's a matter of choice; it seems to be the satisfactory level for separating the alcohol from the mash and water."

Q. "How many runs do commercial distillers use?"

A. "Maybe two and that's a 'continuous run' method."

Q. "No pots?"

A. "No pots per se, but lots of pipes."

Q. "What will happen if a person tries tasting this second run booze now?"

A. "Not much. He'll taste lousy booze with a taste of yeast."

Q. "How about third run booze?"

A. "It'll be better, but not quite done."

Q. "And then, fourth run?"

A. "Properly done, fourth run booze will be tasteless and odorless, and will sparkle when it comes out of the still."

Q. "What's the temperature for the third run? Same as the second run?"

A. "Oh, no! The maximum temperature for the third run is lower: 84°C."

Preparing the Bottles

The finished booze must have *clean containers*, for the drinkers will judge the liquor primarily by its taste and, secondly, by its color. (The average person, for example, can taste or smell chlorine in as little as three parts per million.)

The bottles (in this case, jugs) are cleaned with the vinegar/salt/water solution. All traces of the syrup are removed, and the bottles are then allowed to dry in the sunlight. Each of the caps should have its cardboard insert pried out and discarded, as these inserts carry an objectionable taste.

After the clean jugs are filled with the pure alcohol, cover the mouths with common kitchen wrap and screw the cap down over the plastic.

In general, the alcohol shouldn't come in contact with anything other than its glass container. Once all the bottles pass the taste and odor tests, they are ready for use.

The third run is finished, with the clear fluid sitting in two clean plastic barrels.

THE FOURTH RUN

The still is once more cleaned in preparation for the fourth and last run. You will see black flecks coming from the cooling coil, as the salt/water/vinegar solution is poured through. The pots and covers are thoroughly scrubbed and rinsed, again and again, until they all taste clean. The pots are filled with the third run and closed, and the heaters are turned on.

Here's another important factor in making good booze! Take the vinegar bottle and place it under the discharge spout. Catch the first cup-and-a-half from each potful during the fourth run.

Set this "stuff" aside. In this material are the fusel oils and higher alcohols that give people hangovers and headaches. This first catch is not fit for drinking; it can, however, be used for washing car parts or starting charcoal fires. Keep it totally separate from your drinking booze. *Separating the fusel oils and higher alcohols is the third secret to making good booze!*

This last run has to be watched closely for two reasons. The distilled alcohol will come out very fast now, so you have to watch closely and change the jugs frequently. Also, the cooling tank will become hot and tend to overheat. From the repeated third and fourth runs, the water is now steadily warming. Your first warning sign will be vapor rising from the water's surface. Your next sign if the water is allowed to get too hot will be alcohol vapor coming out the spout. That is dangerous! If that should happen to you, *don't touch those switches and cause a spark!* Merely go to the freezer and get some ice cubes. Throw them into the tank and watch the fluid flow resume from the discharge port. Reduce the heat.

If all goes well, the odorless, tasteless alcohol will come out 95 percent pure, or 190 proof; 100 percent, or 200 proof, alcohol (also known as *absolute* alcohol) is not seen in nature. Alcohol seems to like that 5 percent

moisture. Our temperature for the fourth run is 82°C.
Remember the following:
The first run is cut off at 96°C.
The second run is cut off at 94°C.
The third run is cut off at 84°C.
The fourth run is cut off at 82°C.
You might wonder if you're getting all the alcohol
out of the mash at these temperatures. You're getting
most of it. These temperatures are 1°C. lower than
actual maximum temperatures for these runs, in order to
account for any thermometer variances. Some people
may attempt to "push the temps" a little. But, a word of
warning: Once that booze is burned (you can taste it),
there's little you can do.

INTERRUPTIONS

Let's assume you're in the middle of a potful that is
cooking, and, for some reason, you have to leave. What
are you going to do?
It won't hurt the pot or the liquid if you shut off the
power and leave for a while, but don't *ever* leave a
cooking pot unattended! When you return, you may
resume the cooking by turning the power on again.
Your time schedule may be goofed up if you are a time-
conscious person and concerned about that. Otherwise,
to leave the power off and the pot(s) idle for a couple of
hours won't hurt.
Leaving the pots idle for longer than that, however,
can cause problems. To leave the pots loaded, let's say,

overnight, is asking for a bad batch of booze. The alcohol may pick up an off taste from the aluminum cookers.

If you're going to be gone for any length of time, it's best to dump the pots out.

4.

Bourbon, Gin, and Other Flavored Liquors

The four runs have gone smoothly; you've run off a batch and now have 22 gallon jugs of clear fluid.

Is it ready to drink? No, not quite, for you are at a decision point. Do you wish to drink it flavorless (like moonshine) or do you want to make it into something more tasteful?

BOURBON

Let's see how to make sugar alky into bourbon. The solution to that is easy; all you have to do is add charred oak chips to the *uncut, clear* booze in the selected jugs. The action is quite similar to keeping whiskey in oak casks for that added flavor. The chips will be allowed to sit and soak until the alcohol takes on a color darker than what is desired. The alcohol will then be filtered

27

through cotton and prepared for the next step.
What? You can't drink it yet?
No, not quite. There's one more step before you can present the product as respectable. Alcohol right out of a still is *uncut* booze (190 proof) and is not the most pleasant for the average drinker. The connoisseur would snort at us! You need to legitimately cut the alcohol with water or it will "burn" the prepared drink.

Right now, you've got 95 percent ethyl alcohol and 5 percent water. The next step is to reset the jug levels to half full and then you're ready to cut the booze down to 86 to 90 proof.

Adding water at this time will cause a reaction to take place. This is called *hydration*, a process in which the water molecules cluster around the molecules of alcohol. The individual jugs will become very warm. I instruct people to wait at least eight hours before drinking this cut alcohol; by then, the hydration is complete. The alcohol will taste smooth and pleasant.

OTHER LIQUORS

What else can be made from uncut, clear alcohol? Just about any liquor you desire can be made or mixed.

Would you like gin? Merely purchase gin essence (from a wholesale liquor supply house or specialty shop) and add a few drops. Bingo! You've got gin! Now, cut the booze to 86 to 90 proof.

The same goes for vodka, scotch, rye, and others. The color may not change (label your bottles), but the taste will certainly be there.

Q. "Can the booze spoil where it is?"

A. "No."

Q. "Is this alcohol dangerous?"

A. "If spilled and ignited, yes."

Q. "Can I make beer with this alcohol?"

A. "Not really."

Q. "Wine?"

A. "No, get grapes or grape juice."

Q. "Is drinking this homemade booze much like drinking store-bought booze?"

A. "There will be less bite to this, and the first time you drink it, you may become *very relaxed*. Try it when you have a couple of days off!"

Q. "How about the orange-flavored liqueur?"

A. "That's an easy one! Take a wide-mouthed gallon jug and fill it halfway with uncut clear. Tie a string around an orange and suspend it *over (not in)* the alcohol. Cap the jug and let it sit until the orange shrivels up. Repeat the process. After the second or third orange has dried out, remove it. At the kitchen stove, prepare a simple syrup (you can find a recipe for this in any cookbook--it is basically water and sugar cooked down until thickened) and then add the syrup to the orange-flavored alcohol. You now have orange-flavored liqueur."

Q. "How about a coffee-flavored liqueur?"

A. "Merely select the coffee beans you prefer and have them ground. Pour the coffee beans into the uncut, clear alcohol and let them sit. After a week or so, filter the fluid and, again, add as much syrup as you like."

In making full use of your uncut alcohol, you may create any drinks you and your friends may enjoy. Any fruit, nut, or beverage base can be used for a liqueur flavor. Generally speaking, the liqueurs I have tasted were *not cut* with water and were therefore very potent! I would advise you to cut your liqueurs down to about 90 proof *after* flavoring them.

With a wide variety of homemade liqueurs at hand, it can be fun if you invite a friend over to taste all of them. Merely take his car keys from him, and let him start to sample! I believe I got to six or seven drinks before I was out on the floor! Another idea is to take some uncut clear and set it in the freezer for a few months. It will thicken, much like a syrup, and be a real challenge to the "professional" drinker!

5.

Safeguards and Other Advice

We've already covered the basic safety rules in making booze: no smoking and no drinking. Later, we mentioned the "secrets" of making good booze:

1. Keep the equipment clean.
2. Don't exceed the maximum temperatures.
3. Remove the fusel oils at the start of the fourth run.

There are a few other considerations you should be aware of.

THE SELF-DESIGNATED EXPERT

Every neighborhood has one, and it won't be long before he discovers you have a still and has to come over with some free advice. Yes, he's the one who has five credits in college chemistry, and he's there to tell you how to cook the booze. Quite naturally, if you're turning out a good beverage, he's there to take the credit! The best thing you can do with this type of clown is to escort him out the door!

You'll probably run into the second "bird" too: He's the joker who comes out from under a rock, suggesting that you should put a "reflux tower" on top of your still. Then, he assures you, more alcohol will be generated. This column or tube device is often filled with some exotic metal wool or pellets that enable you to obtain a specific organic reaction. It's a damned fool idea and dangerous! (Unless, of course, you're willing to experiment on your friends.)

The best course for you to take is to merely claim ignorance of any still and escort the jerk out the door.

SAFEGUARDS AND OTHER ADVICE

To protect yourself and your still, it's always best and safest to keep quiet about its existence. It'll never hurt you if you say nothing about any booze-making rig you may have.

Virtually every neighborhood has a busybody or gossip. One of them might be prone to calling the authorities just to be antagonistic.

Usually, your main problem during booze-making is to reduce or confine the smell. The smell of carelessly dumped hot mash can creep across a neighborhood and yet, with the use of a soft hose and rags, 250 gallons of hot mash can be dumped with hardly a whiff in the air.

As far as procuring your supplies, if you work in a grocery wholesale house or bakery, you are indeed lucky. Other than that, you might want to buy your sugar from different suppliers or wholesalers—seldom at the same place twice. The same goes for the yeast: buy at totally different places or have someone else do the buying for you. Buying large quantities of sugar or yeast in one place can be a tipoff that you're making your own booze.

THE HOBBY COOKER

Are you the type of guy who merely wants to cook off a little in his apartment? Sure, that's workable. You may elect to set one mash barrel and then, later, one cooker on the stove.

It'll work quite satisfactorily; the only thing is that you'll have to sit there and "mind the baby." Smaller cookers require closer watching, for they will come up to maximum temperature in a hurry! Just like any other still, there is no room for open flames. And yet, all the other safeguards still apply.

MIXING GOOD DRINKS
FOR A SUCCESSFUL PARTY

Two rules for having a good party are:
1. Don't push the drinks on your guests.
2. Don't ever load up the drinks.

Serve drinks to the people who respond to your invitation and then only serve single-shot drinks (unless someone demands a "double").

If you're bent on making a good impression, make use of the "trick" of washing the glasses beforehand with the vinegar-saltwater mixture and then following with generous rinses. That will remove most (if not all) tastes and residues.

When mixing a drink, always put the ice in first. Next, pour the single shot of booze over the ice. Finally, add the water or mix. Stay in that order and you'll make a lot of guests happy.

Unless you are running low on ice, give each refill new ice. (The people who want to get loaded will ask for lots of ice, which takes up more room in the glass and leaves less room for mixer—no matter.) In any event, merely serve single-shot drinks and the party will go on for a longer time.

FINAL WORDS

There you have it: all my "secrets" about cooking and serving *good* booze. I am confident you will have a lot of fun. Admittedly, there's a degree of hard work involved, especially in getting set up. After that, you'll find (as I have) that it's quite an enjoyable experience! Bottoms up!

Appendix
Equipment
and Supplies

EQUIPMENT

New plastic garbage can with tight-fitting cover
Pressure cooker
Centigrade thermometer
Pail
Eight-foot copper tubing
Two copper fittings and a nut
Glass jugs and caps
O-ring (for thermometer)
Optional drain valve
Optional electric hot plates (up to 5,000 watts)
Optional water tank
Bottle brush
Two plastic funnels
Thermometer tube (to keep thermometer warm)
Optional electric pump and hose

SUPPLIES

Sugar (approximately 16 lbs. to yield one gallon of alcohol)

Raw water (at room temperature)

Fresh yeast (1/3 cup per gallon of finished alcohol)

Salt

Vinegar

Medicinal oil

Plastic wrap

Aluminum wool or plastic scrub pad

Real cotton (for filtering the booze)

Charred oak chips (optional)

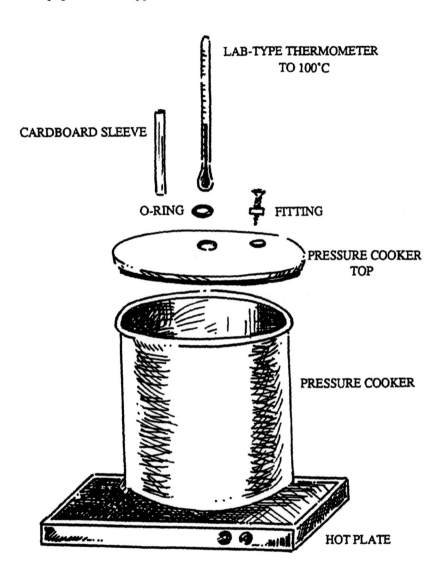

LAB-TYPE THERMOMETER
TO 100°C

CARDBOARD SLEEVE

O-RING

FITTING

PRESSURE COOKER
TOP

PRESSURE COOKER

HOT PLATE

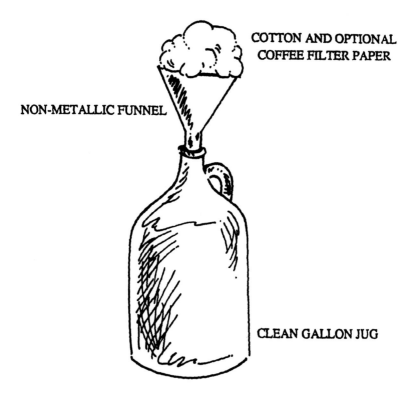

COTTON AND OPTIONAL
COFFEE FILTER PAPER

NON-METALLIC FUNNEL

CLEAN GALLON JUG

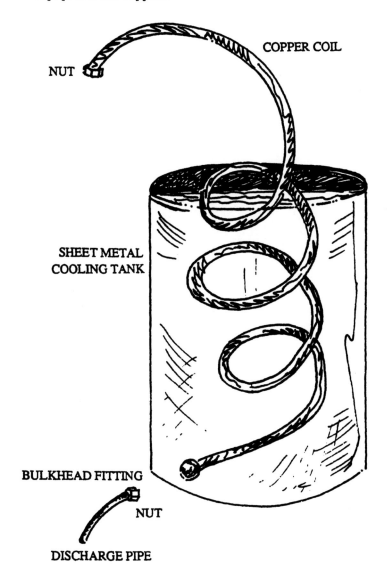

NUT

COPPER COIL

SHEET METAL
COOLING TANK

BULKHEAD FITTING

NUT

DISCHARGE PIPE